A ^{mostly} KIDS' GUIDE TO NAPLES MARCO ISLAND & THE EVERGLADES

KAREN T. BARTLETT

Mostly Kids Guides LLC

First published February 2015 by
Mostly Kids Guides LLC
6141 Pelican Bay Blvd; Naples, FL 34108

10 9 8 7 6 5 4 3 2 1

Cover design and illustrations by Terri Rickman
Inside design by Judy Fernandez and Sharon Hood
Maps by Randall Simmons and Judy Fernandez
Photography by Karen T. Bartlett except where otherwise credited
Research Assistant: Linda Jacobson
Copy Editor: Randall Simmons

To purchase additional copies of this book, to schedule an event, or for information about special volume discounts, contact Karen T. Bartlett
(239) 595-9026
mostlykidsguides@gmail.com
🐦 @kidsguides 📘 Mostly Kids Guides
www.mostlykidsguides.com

ISBN 978-0-9909731-0-2
ISBN 978-0-9909731-1-9 Kindle
ISBN 978-0-9909731-2-6 all other digital media

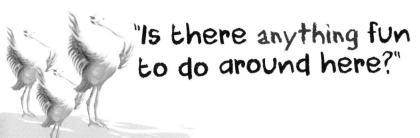

"Is there anything fun to do around here?"

"Are you kidding me?"

Where does a 300-pound prehistoric sea turtle dig her nest?
Is there really **buried treasure** in the Ten Thousand Islands?
When is a palm tree **not** a palm tree?

Is it true that there are angels and ghosts in the swamp,
and **grass-eating cows** living underwater?
(Clue: well, sort of! You'll have to read this book to find out.)

This book is dedicated to **Sarah Rose Bartlett** and Christopher Y. Bartlett, the two most awesome kids on the planet. And I'm not saying that just because **I'm their mom.** When they were small and we began our adventures, there was no handy book to give us the **inside scoop**, tell us about all the great **festivals, parades** and **free stuff** to do.

So here's your **treasure map** to **cool places** to go, outrageously exciting things to do, secrets revealed, and stuff that's almost **too bizarre to be true.** but it is!

It's **supposed to be for kids**, but I guess **we can't stop the grownups** from taking a peek. Besides, you'll need someone to drive you, right?

Happy adventuring!

Karen T. Bartlett
Adventurer in Chief

Bird Legs and bizarre beaks

← Good stuff for a school report!

Wading Birds, like ibis and herons, have long necks and long skinny legs. They fish with sharp pointy **beaks like tweezers**. A roseate spoonbill is a wading bird, too, but instead of tweezers, it scoops up its food with the handy spoon at the end of its beak!

Shore Birds, like sandpipers, **skitter along** the water's edge, poking in the sand for dinner.

Sea Birds, like gulls and pelicans, swoop down and **dive for their dinner**.

ibis has a → tweezer beak

Green flash!

A bright green glow sometimes happens when the last tip of the sun drops into the sea. Lots of people have seen it. Maybe you will. Remember: **never stare into the sun**.

Live shelling: Don't do it!

If you find a shell with the creature still inside, or a starfish that's still soft– even if it's washed up on the beach and not feeling well, toss it back! Live shells die and get REALLY smelly. Also, it's against the law. Empty shells are fine to take!

"Even if the creature is already dead and stinky, don't take it! Why? It's dinner for crabs and birds!"

Cowabunga! It's a manatee!

In ancient times, drunken sailors saw manatees and thought they were mermaids. Nowadays, people call them **sea cows**. Why? Because they're bulky and cow-like! Also, they chew grass. Sea grass, that is.

Manatees move very slowly (you might too, if you weighed almost 2,000 pounds!) so their worst enemies are boat propellers.

manatee: stockbyte/Thinkstock

Boats have to slow down in manatee habitats.

Boardwalk Secrets
Boardwalks help protect the swamps, beaches, preserves and prairies. Look down and see what might be looking up at you!

Free, Free, Free!
Tons of awesome happenings are totally free. See how many you can find in this book!

What color is your Key Lime pie?

Key limes make yellow juice. If your server brings a slice of bright green Key lime pie, somebody in the kitchen had fun with food coloring.

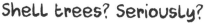

Shell trees? Seriously?

Get close and you'll see what's really going on here. Certain sea snails drill holes in small shells to slurp out the animal inside. It's said that if you hang a shell on a tree, you're sure to return some day.

Find the tree in this picture ➜

Who knew? A palm tree is just a blade of grass. It's a bit more complicated than that, but its true! Palms aren't trees at all. They're actually closer relatives of onions, or the grass in your garden.

← grass

← tree

Pink flamingo? NOT!

"If you see a pink flamingo around here, it's either in the zoo or a plastic souvenir. The pink bird you see around here is me: roseate spoonbill!"

Zebra Longwing:

It's Florida's state butterfly. The name fits, don't you think?

NAPLES
TREASURES & ADVENTURES ON LAND & SEA

The thing about Naples is, you're always near a beach. Wherever you are, practically all you have to do is head west. Soon, you'll be wiggling your toes in the sand, building sand castles and picking up pretty shells.

But wait till you see what else! You can climb a treehouse just like in the movies, meet a pirate (or be one!), ride a horse, go skateboarding and a gazillion other things.

Beach Time!

Lots of people say Naples has the **most beautiful beaches in America**, including Dr. Beach (real name, Stephen Leatherman). He's a coastal ecologist who travels around the country picking his favorite beaches!

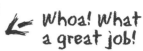 Whoa! What a great job!

"The Naples Pier and other county beaches have kids' life jackets to borrow, free!"

Meet Me at the Pier!

Number One Rule for Naples visitors: you have to walk to the **very end of the Naples Pier** at least once to watch the sun set. Okay, we made that up, but it would be very sad if you didn't. Besides the sunsets and super-fun beach, there are always **dolphins, pelicans, sea gulls and ospreys** hanging out, watching the fishermen catch the big ones. There is a beach volleyball court for the older kids, and a snack bar on the pier.

After you've played yourself silly at the Pier, then what? Why, go looking for more! Here are **five amazing beach parks** to get you started.

Lowdermilk Park

You're sure to make new friends on this wide family beach, which also has **playgrounds**, sand volleyball, a covered **food pavilion** and shady picnic tables.

Big snook! Catch and release only!

Clam Pass Park

Ride the tram through the shady mangrove forest and come out on the most beautiful beach ever! There's all kinds of beach equipment to rent, a snack deck, and lots of wildlife!

Vanderbilt Beach Park

This is another awesome place people go to watch the sunset. It's also great for sandcastle building, swimming and paddling. Food and convenience shops are nearby.

Delnor-Wiggins Pass State Park

has picnic areas with grills, ranger activities, fantastic fishing spots, food concessions, kayak and paddleboard rentals, beach umbrellas, and even a fire tower to climb! Entrance is free with a Florida State Parks annual pass.

Barefoot Beach Preserve Park

Have a picnic, an adventure with a ranger, go kayaking, watch the pelicans diving for their lunch, have lunch yourself, find some shells, play in the water, and then start all over again!

Visitors: buy beach parking permits from Collier County Parks & Recreation.

Giant Prehistoric Sea Turtles!

Every spring, giant loggerhead sea turtles swim to the same beaches where they were born to lay their eggs.

Markus Hennig

They crawl out of the sea at night and use their huge flippers to dig nests. This is hard work for the mother turtle. When she hatched, she weighed only one ounce. **Now she weighs about 300 pounds!**

Afterward, she crawls v-e-r-y slowly back to the sea. Every morning, turtle specialists patrol the beaches to mark the new nests.

Loggerhead tracks look like giant tractor tires!

Here's the most exciting part!

All the baby loggerheads hatch at the same time! They run as fast as their tiny legs can take them to the sea, because crabs and birds love to eat them for breakfast.

Turtle specialists rescue any hatchlings stuck in the nests, and count the empty shells. That can add up to 100,000 eggs a year!

Everyone loves the turtle biologists! Come to the beach early one morning during nesting time and watch them work!

When a baby girl turtle grows up, in about 35 years, she'll swim back thousands of miles (from other oceans, even!) to lay her eggs. How can she remember the exact beach where she was born?

It's a mystery!

At the **Conservancy of Southwest Florida**, you can peek into the hospital for **injured wildlife** and **orphaned baby animals**, see injured shore birds getting well in their **rehab pool**, and meet animal "ambassadors" of all kinds. You also can watch for gopher tortoises on nature trails, see manatees on a free 45-minute river cruise or join a guided **kayak paddle** through the mangroves.

The Dalton Discovery Center has more than 100 animals and interactive exhibits. You get to push buttons and watch splendiferous things happen on the beaches, in the mangroves and the Everglades.

splendiferous things!

You can feel around in the touch tank for **live horseshoe crabs and sea stars**, and then see **Betsy, the loggerhead sea turtle** who's growing up and will one day be released into the wild.

The Conservancy has awesome one- and two-day camps for kids in grades 2 to 5. Attention, kids under 5: at **Lil' Explorers** you can be a junior veterinarian, build a creature tunnel called a burrow, and have fun with nature crafts, stories and activities.

What's up at the Naples Zoo? Besides the giraffes, we mean. They're WAY up there, but they love to bend down and let you feed them! You also can cruise around the **primate islands**, where apes, monkeys and lemurs hang out in the trees, and see fun shows in the **Safari Canyon** theater. You'll smile at the bears having lunch at their backyard picnic table, see serious chomping action in **Alligator Bay** at feeding time, and get practically nose-to-nose with cobras, vipers and more at the **Snakes Alive! Presentation.**

Meet the keepers who care for the animals, from **lions and tigers** to s-lo-w sloths and prickly porcupines. Show up on an animal's birthday or a holiday and you might see it clawing open its presents!

Whoa! Who knew?

A giraffe's tongue is black, not pink, and can be 20 inches long! If you think that's something, wait till you see the anteater! And by the way, don't get into a race with a cheetah. Why? It can run 100 feet per second.

FREE ALERT! The first Saturday every month is free for Collier County residents.

13

Shy Wolves, Screaming Cats

Some people try to raise a baby wolf or snake at home, but when it grows up it isn't so cuddly anymore. Sometimes they abandon these **exotic pets** or keep them in tiny cages and stop loving them. Naples has **two sanctuaries** where rescued exotic pets can live happy lives. They're both **free to visit** with advance reservations.

Forget about the Big Bad Wolf! You'll love the wolves and wolfdogs at the Shy Wolf Sanctuary. They arrived sad and hurt, but now get lots of love and care.

Shy Wolf Sanctuary also has prairie dogs, coyotes, foxes and more.

Can you tell a wolf's howl from a coyote's? Come listen! Wolves howl longer and sound deeper.

Want to hug a skunk? Pet an iguana? Cuddle with a four foot-long python? You can meet horses, pot-bellied pigs and more than 130 other critters (and even pet some) at Kowiachobee Animal Preserve. The name comes from a Native American word meaning **"big screaming cat."** You'll see tigers, cougars and other big cats, but there's not much screaming going on, except maybe by the parrots.

P.S. Don't worry; the skunk isn't stinky.

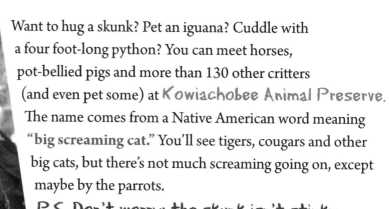

5th Avenue South

When archaeologists started digging around Naples' most famous shopping street, can you guess what they found out? **It once was a prehistoric Indian canoe trail!** Back then, it was a shortcut from Naples Bay to the Gulf of Mexico, and it still is. There may be no more fierce warriors paddling dugout canoes, but 5th Avenue South gets very exciting, especially when they close off the whole street for a parade or festival. **Oh, what colors you'll see** when artists cover the street with awesome chalk paintings. And wait till you see the Christmas magic in Sugden Plaza!

Educational Chocolate?

Imagine spending a whole hour popping in and out of ice cream, cupcake, fudge and cookie stores and having a taste at every one? You can! Tell the grownups that the **Naples Chocolate Stroll** is educational. What kind of stuff will you learn? Well, when movies were filmed in black & white, they used melted chocolate to look like blood.

eeeew!

Q: What do cannibals eat for dessert?

A: Chocolate covered aunts, of course!

Cambier Park

We know it's not nice to brag, but the new playground at Cambier Park downtown is beyond awesome! There also are **movies on the lawn,** free shows and festivals, ping-pong and pool tables in the community center, and great **tennis** courts where kids can play for just $5.

What's-what and what's-where in Naples? Hop aboard the trolley and find out! The tour guides tell **hilarious secrets** about Naples people, places and creatures. You can hop off (and back on) at any of the **21 stops** whenever you'd like, for lunch, souvenir shopping or beach play.

Naples Trolley

Dog Parks, Too!

Your pooch is welcome in Cambier Park on a leash, but dogs can romp around off-leash at nearby **Central Bark**, the City of Naples Dog Park, or in Veterans Community Park's **Rover Run** (North Naples). Big and little dogs have separate playgrounds. Check city and county requirements for tags and registration.

It's the **pet-friendliest** street in town! They say any pet is welcome–even your pet llama! Dogs love sitting with their people at the sidewalk cafes, and shopping for treats at the **Saturday farmer's market**. They even have their own costume parade in January. *super fun!*

During the holidays, 3rd Street South is a magical wonderland with trees all sparkly with white lights. **Santa** and the **Fairy Snowmother** show up, and it even snows!

How about a horse-drawn carriage ride to the Naples Pier? Meet your white horse, Dixie, the star of **Charlene's Classic Carriages**, near the 3rd Street gazebo most nights from November to April.

17

What's up on Naples Bay?

Every cool water and land adventure you can imagine, that's what! Check it out at these four big marinas: **Tin City**, **Port of Naples Marina**, **Bayfront**, and **City Dock** at Crayton Cove.

The water shuttle *Blue Pelican* is a cool way to get around between the marinas and downtown. An all-day kid's ticket is just $5.

Oyster Shacks

Once upon a time, clam and oyster

boats chugged up to the docks on Naples Bay to unload their catch. Their **oyster-shucking shacks** smelled pretty stinky. When the shellfish beds dried up and the factories closed, someone had the brilliant idea to paint the tin shacks bright colors, connect them together and make it a fun place to shop and eat. Now, Tin City smells more like cookies and burgers than stinky oyster shells.

Shop for **awesome souvenirs**, like magic tricks, chocolate alligators, funny t-shirts, and who knows what else. Have lunch on the docks and watch the boats pass by. Be sure to try an **outrageously yummy treat** at the MonKey Bread Factory.

Double Sunshine

On Saturday mornings, kids go free on this big double decker boat's super-fun **dolphin sightseeing cruise**, with a scavenger hunt and prizes. *Double Sunshine* has five cool sails each day the rest of the week, too.

Naples Princess

Sail into the sunset like a bazillionaire on the fancy 105-foot long yacht *Naples Princess.* You can see the **mansions of Port Royal** and watch for dolphins through the big windows inside on the main deck, or **al fresco** on the top deck.

Naples Princess has day and sunset cruises, fun party cruises, and you can even have lunch or dinner on board.

Invite all the aunts, uncles, cousins and grandparents for a family reunion or an **extra-special birthday party!** You'll get to meet the captain, of course, and at the end of the cruise, look for the souvenir picture of you on the gangway. Get on board at Port of Naples Marina.

Kids age 2 and under are free!

QUIZ
al fresco means
a) a kind of smoothie
b) a city in California
c) in the fresh air

Answer: c

Port of Naples Marina is also a great place to rent paddleboards, Jet Skis, kayaks and family size sightseeing boats. You can also sign up for a private fishing trip or a Jet Ski tour. You must be at least age 14 to drive your own, but even little kids can ride with a grownup!

istockphoto/Thinkstock

Helmet goes on
before tour starts.

Self-Balancing Human Transporter ← huh?

That's the real name for a Segway, a two-wheeled motorized thingy that's smaller than a bicycle and easier than a skateboard. **You ride standing up,** balancing like a gyroscope. (Puh-leez don't ask how a gyroscope works).

If you're at least age14 and 100 pounds, it's a sweet way to tool around the historic waterfront and Old Naples. Join an escorted Segway tour at **Naples Transportation & Tours** near Tin City, or at **Extreme Family Fun Spot** at Naples Bayfront.

Thrills and Chills!

If you're at least 38 inches tall and love fast boats, check out **Jet Boat Naples.** The 24-passenger jet boat *Odin* is like a roller coaster on water. Do you dare raise both hands in the air?

Or, for something more peaceful...

Even little kids love the **Sunset Family Fishing Cruise** aboard the *Naples Explorer.* You bring the snacks; the crew does the rest. They'll even fillet your catch. Sweet!

Sign up at the Pure Naples hut, Tin City.

Pure Naples

Crayton Cove

Pizza, Sailboats and a Sea Creature!

Sea creature selfie!

There's a humongous flagpole in the middle of the road where 12th Avenue South runs smack into the City Dock. Around it, there's an ice cream and **pizza** place, three more **restaurants**, cool **souvenir** shops and art **galleries**, and a studio to make your own **pottery**. It's fun to walk along the dock and check out the big sailboats, yachts and fishing charters.

Sweet Liberty

Oooh! Aaah! That's what people say when this **53-foot catamaran** sails by on its sightseeing, sunset, dolphin watch and shelling cruises.

Kids love to hang out on the open deck, watching for dolphins, raptors and desert islands. There's also a snack bar and a comfy **saloon** inside the main deck, with tables to have lunch or sort your shells. Guess what? If you don't see a dolphin the whole trip, **you get to take another cruise, free!**

"Back in the old days, "saloon" was real sailor talk for the boat's living room."

Collier County Parks & Recreation

Slide! Zoom! Plume and Flume!

If you've been to a more exciting water park than the **Sun & Fun Lagoon**, it was probably on another planet. You've got water-dumping buckets, water pistols, four pools and a lazy river, and (if you're at least 48" tall) five super water slides, including a 38-foot tower! **Turtle Cove** is for kids 5 to 12, and the littlest ones get their own tadpole pool.

Woo hoo!

Can U Dig It?

Sun & Fun Lagoon is part of **North Collier Regional Park**, which also has baseball fields, soccer fields, a big playground with slides, swings, big rocks to climb, squiggly poles, and climbing structures. It's called Can U Dig It, because there's even a Calusa fossil dig!

Mini Golf

A hole-in-one gets you a free game at **Coral Cay Adventure Golf**, where you putt your way through a cave, a coral reef, and waterfalls on two 18-hole courses.

Discover Scuba!

Kids age 10 and older can get scuba-certified in five days or less at **Naples Marina & Excursions**. Not 10 yet? Start with the Bubblemaker class. They also have fun fishing charters (even spearfishing!), kayaking, paddleboarding and kids' camps.

Garden-Licious!

Who said a garden is just a bunch of flowers? Here's what you can do at Naples Botanical Garden: Play in the water fountain. Climb an awesome treehouse. Visit a cave and waterfall. Build a sand castle. Discover all sorts of bizarre things that are definitely NOT flowers in the **Hidden Garden**, including a toilet clogged with flowers. Seriously!

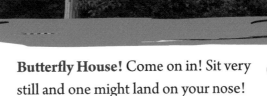

Butterfly House! Come on in! Sit very still and one might land on your nose!

The **Cracker House** is a cool kid-size playhouse. You can plant flowers, dig weeds, or water the organic vegetables. Pay attention–surprises are everywhere! Can you spot the **tree wearing striped socks?**

Dogs are welcome in the Garden three days a week. They have their own private entrance and get treats, too!

Drop in any Saturday or Sunday between 10:30 a.m. and 3 p.m. and be a **W.O.N.D.E.R. kid**. It's a different adventure every month. Even grownups love it!

Do you love to ride horses?

Saddle Up!

Even first-timers love the gentle horseback tour with **M&H Stables** at the edge of the deep and mysterious Picayune Strand State Forest. See if you can spot a shy deer, coyote or bobcat.

Do you Shred, Grind and Ollie?

If you know that sometimes a bowl has nothing to do with cereal, and a snake is not a reptile, **The Edge Johnny Nocera Skate Park** is your dream place! This huge skate/bike park has awesome wood and concrete ramps for beginners to star athletes age 14 up, with alternating skate and bike sessions.

You know what to do!

Feel Like taking a bike ride?

Check out the new **Gordon River Greenway!** The paved nature trail follows the Gordon River, beside the Zoo and the Conservancy. Watch for a great horned owl, bald eagle, raccoon or even a fox! **Rent a bike** at one of Naples' bicycle shops, or join a group with **Naples Bicycle Tours**. Helmets, water and snacks are included.

istockphoto/Thinkstock

Climb a wall! Be a Tortoise!

Golisano Children's Museum of Naples (C'mon) is supposed to be for kids, but who are they fooling? Parents, grandparents, aunts and uncles have a blast! Toddlers under age 3 have their own play lots. Bigger kids can go fishing at the pretend pier or manage a pretend restaurant. You can climb a wall or a giant banyan tree, be a Naples Trolley driver or a meteorologist in the TV studio. In Mother Nature's House, autumn brings falling leaves, and summer brings a tropical storm, lightning and all! And be sure to check out the igloo! **ADULTS KEEP OUT** of Curious Kids, where teens and pre-teens do scientific experiments, invent, write, design and build things.

"Ever wondered how boy alligators make girl gators fall in love with them? Here's the secret: we make bubbles! If two of us are interested in a pretty girl, you wouldn't believe the huge, noisy, splashy show we give her. Whoever makes the biggest bubbles wins."

Nice → idea

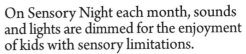
On Sensory Night each month, sounds and lights are dimmed for the enjoyment of kids with sensory limitations.

Old Train Depot

The Naples Depot Museum started more than a hundred years ago as a Seaboard Air Line Railway train station. Inside are other kinds of transportation from the past: a Seminole dugout canoe, a mule wagon, an antique swamp buggy, a 1955 Chevy Bel Air, and even the front end of an Army Air Force plane. Be sure to take a selfie at the **100-year-old red caboose!**

All Aboard!

Also at the Depot is the **Naples Train Museum**. Only grownups pay to get in. Watch **Thomas the Tank** and other miniature Lionel trains chug around the model city. Push buttons and watch things happen. Then, go outside and hop aboard the mini-train, pulled by a **real diesel locomotive**. That's free, too! Check ahead for dates and times.

Oldest House

In Europe, a hundred-year-old house is practically new. But in Naples, that's ANCIENT! When pioneers built **Palm Cottage** near the Naples Pier in 1895, using a mortar of sand and seashells, Naples wasn't even born yet. It's extra-nice all decorated for the holidays.

Holocaust Museum

With letters, family pictures, artifacts and peoples' stories, The Holocaust Museum and Education Center helps visitors understand the horrible crimes of Hitler's Nazi regime, to make sure that such things are never allowed to happen again. The museum has public tours (most appropriate for kids over 10) and can arrange private family tours.

Step Right Into History!

How would you like to zoom through about 10,000 years of Southwest Florida history in one day? At the **Old Florida Festival**, you'll meet prehistoric Calusa Indians, Spanish Conquistadors, World War II soldiers and other historic characters. They're re-enactors of course! You'll also meet real Seminole Indians, make your own Calusa mask and other cool stuff, see Native American dances, watch battles–even visit a battlefield hospital–and tons of other action.

↗ Happens each spring at the Collier County Museum.

Indian, Mastadon (below) courtesy Collier County Museum

Prehistoric Mastodon, War Tank and More!

The Collier County Museum is fun to visit all year. Step inside beneath the giant prehistoric mastodon bones and check out the interactive exhibits inside. Outside, you'll find a real 33-ton World War II Sherman tank, the "Old Number 2" steam locomotive once used for logging in the cypress swamps, a Seminole war fort and a Calusa Indian camp. **It's totally free!**

Where do sailing champions get their start?

At sailing schools and camps! Ask the Naples Community Sailing Center about classes, or take a lesson on Lake Avalon at **Sugden Regional Park**, or just go and watch a **regatta** on a Naples beach!

Besides sailing, here's what else you can do at Sugden Park: Ride bikes around the lake. Learn to water ski. Watch a ski show. Swim, fish, kayak, canoe or paddleboat. See what's flitting around the butterfly garden. Climb on the cool playground structure. Have a picnic. And don't miss the GINORMOUS ice cream social with games, ski shows and fireworks on the Fourth of July!

Rev it Up!

1966 Porsche 906 Carrera.
1974 Jorgensen Eagle.
1966 Ford GT40. 1995 McLaren F1.
If these names get your heart racing, head straight to The Revs Institute to see them,

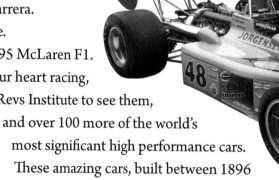

and over 100 more of the world's most significant high performance cars. These amazing cars, built between 1896 and 1995, aren't displayed behind ropes, but right out there in the galleries so you can see every awesome detail. Best for older kids. Tickets and tours are by reservation.

Courtesy of The Revs Institute

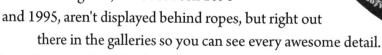

Most Outrageous Canoe Race on the Planet!

Each May, crowds line up on the City Dock to watch **The Great Dock Canoe Race**, where some of the racers disguise their canoes to look like everything from cheeseburgers to zombies.

Yep, there's plenty of tipping over!

On Stage and in the Street

Do you love to dance, act, or play an instrument?
Kids like you perform around Naples all year long!
Catch KidzAct Youth Theatre shows at Sugden Community Theatre,
and the amazing **Naples Youth Orchestra** at Artis—Naples. During the holidays, several local kids dance in *The Nutcracker* with Miami City Ballet's professional dancers at Artis—Naples, and there's super-fun singing and dancing in *Nutcracker Goes Pop!* at Sugden. And oh, those parades! You'll see why our marching bands are world famous!

Muck, Mud and the Sippy Hole

If it's not a truck, a motorcycle, a racecar, an airplane or a boat, what in the world IS it?
Well, a swamp buggy, invented right here on the edge of the Everglades, could be
all these things rolled into one bizarro vehicle that can slog through the wildest
swamps and boonies. Three weekends a year, you can watch these monster
buggies race around the mucky **Mile O' Mud** at the Florida Sports Park.
Sometimes they sink so low that all you see is the driver's helmet.

↙ Noise alert!

The Swamp Buggy Races are loud and crazy. At the end, the
Swamp Buggy Queen gets dunked in the yucky Sippy Hole wearing
her crown, gown and all! There's fairgrounds food, souvenirs, and of course, Swampy the mascot!
Each fall you can see Swampy and the monster swamp buggies in a parade right down U.S. 41.

She's getting dunked in the Sippy Hole. ↙

IMMOKALEE

Can you guess how to pronounce Immokalee? Well, it **rhymes with broccoli**. It comes from a Seminole Indian word meaning "my home." The Seminoles also once called it Gopher Ridge, because there were so many gopher tortoises.

Before the Seminoles, Immokalee was the hunting ground of the ancient Calusa Indians. Centuries later came the white hunters and pioneer cowmen. Nobody ever called these tough ranchers "cowBOYS," because they were REAL MEN. The wilderness and prairies around Immokalee are still home to deer, black bears and panthers as it was hundreds of years ago.

Deborah Hanson

Tomatoes, Watermelons and More!

Can you believe that 90% of all U.S. winter tomatoes are grown in Florida, and especially in Immokalee? So are juicy watermelons, lettuce, grapefruit, oranges and other fruits and veggies. Families from a wonderful diversity of world cultures plant and harvest these delicious foods we enjoy.

CIW — That stands for Coalition of Immokalee Workers, the famous human rights organization in Immokalee that started the Fair Food Program. CIW is working to improve the lives of farm workers in Florida and beyond.

U-PICK — That means, "you pick your own!" You can, at **Collier Family Farms.** Mmm! ...**strawberries and blueberries** still warm from the sun! To celebrate the opening of the growing season in November, they have pony petting, food, tours and other fun stuff.

Hop into the Orange Jeep!

Take a 90-minute jeep ride through the Collier family's private land of swamps and prairies in Immokalee. Watch for alligators, whitetail deer, the famous Osceola turkey, and other creatures.

Collier Family Farms

RJWiley

Corkscrew Swamp Sanctuary, protected by The National Audubon Society, is the largest strand of **old growth** bald cypress on the continent! Take the boardwalk through the deep, dark forest, over spooky swamp waters, and across wide-open prairies.

← Old growth means hundreds of years old!

What to watch for: alligators, turtles, snakes, deer, ospreys, bald eagles and other raptors. Maybe even a black bear! Can you spot the alligators hiding in the lettuce lake? Check the website for morning storytelling tours and awesome nighttime programs, all free with admission. And definitely be there to celebrate **World Wetlands Day** with music, crafts, a scavenger hunt and dip netting at the pond for all kinds of squiggly things.

"Hey kids! You can't eat this lettuce!"

Corkscrew is big, but it's only one part of **CREW Land and Water Trust**. CREW is HUMONGOUS! It's four times bigger and wraps around the Sanctuary. There are bird rookeries, swamps, prairies, marshes, and hiking trails. At Gate 5, you can hike into a cypress dome, and Gate 1 is a great spot to see wildflowers and butterflies. What's the admission? Zero! Many of the special guided programs are even free.

Hot Air Balloon Festival

Each spring, the Seminole Casino Immokalee invites the whole world, free, to **Balloons Over Paradise** at the tribe's Youth Ranch next door. At sunrise, about 60 huge hot air balloons float into the sky. Afterward, climb into a basket yourself and try a **tethered** balloon ride. There's also a Seminole Indian village, with storytelling, alligator wrestling, food and carnival games.

"Tethered" means it's ← attached to the ground by very long ropes!

Shhh!
A Wilderness Secret

Not many people know about the **Pepper Ranch** wilderness preserve. In October, when it's covered in sunflowers, there's a free **Sunflower Festival**, with hayrides, music, ranch-style food and activities.

On weekends, October through May, you can camp, go hiking, mountain biking, or horseback riding. Bring your own tent, bike or horse, of course!

Real Pioneer Ranch

The Immokalee Pioneer Museum at Roberts Ranch has a cowmen's bunkhouse, sugar cane mill, hide curing house, horse barn and more, just the way they were in pioneer days. **It's free.**

Airboats and Alligators

Stop in at Lake Trafford Marina for a super- thrilling airboat ride. There are tons of gators, birds and other creatures lurking about.

Pirates, Conquistadors and Buried Treasure

The prehistoric **Calusa Indians** were **seafaring warriors** who defended their land against Spanish conquistadors, English explorers and Creek Indians. Spain's first conquistador, Ponce de Leon, was **killed by a Calusa arrow**.

They also were very smart pirates, ambushing **Spanish galleons** carrying Mexican gold. Sea captains told the king of Spain that the Calusa were **cannibals,** but maybe that was just a lame excuse for showing up without any treasure.

Calico Jack's Gold

Around 1719, a hurricane tossed the ship of that **dastardly pirate,** Calico Jack, into the Ten Thousand Islands. What did he find? A **wrecked Spanish treasure ship** loaded with 300,000 gold coins! He **buried the treasure** and went off to plunder more ships. Before he could return for his gold, he was captured and hanged.

Jolly Roger designed by Calico Jack

Treasure on Panther Key?

When another dastardly pirate, Jose Gaspar, got captured by a U.S. warship near here 100 years later, all the crew were killed. Only a a young cabin boy named **Juan Gomez escaped.**

He headed straight to the Ten Thousand Islands. **Could he have known about Calico Jack's treasure?** Juan Gomez lived there as a hermit, fishing and raising goats. He named his island **Panther Key** because panthers kept swimming over to **eat his goats.** He lived to age 122 but he never found the treasure.

Some believe all that gold is still here, waiting to be discovered. **Maybe by you.**

istockphoto/Thinkstock (4)

MARCO ISLAND
ONE GINORMOUS PILE OF SHELLS

Whether or not the Calusa Indians were cannibals, we know one thing: they ate a *lot* of seafood. How do we know? Because Marco Island started as a giant pile of clam, oyster and whelk shells! After a delicious seafood dinner, the Calusas dumped the empty shells into the muddy mangrove roots. A bazillion seafood dinners later, those huge mounds of shells became whole islands. Marco is the largest Calusa Indian garbage dump, (though it's nicer to say shell mound), in the Ten Thousand Islands.

Best recycling ever!

mangrove: Bruce Hitchcock; mask: Rookery Bay

The fierce Calusas used sharpened seashells and sharks' teeth to make powerful weapons. They also carved beautiful masks and sculptures. This small half-panther, half-human carving is in the Smithsonian Institution in Washington, DC, but for more than a thousand years, it was buried in a mucky bog on Marco. Archaeologists call it the **Key Marco Cat**. The people of Marco want it back so badly that they built the **Marco Island Historical Museum**, to give it a safe home. Already the museum has a life-size interactive Calusa village and lots of cool happenings. ← like Pirate Day each January

10,000 Islands? Who's Counting?

It's impossible! Storms wash some away and split others apart. New mangroves pop up practically overnight, making new islands. There might be 10,594 or 25,000. Nobody's actually counting. Of course, you're welcome to try.

Alien spacecraft? **Giant concrete mushrooms?** What are those bizarre white igloo-things poking out of the water at **Cape Romano**? Surprise! They used to be all connected, making one big, strange house on a huge sandy beach. What happened? Hurricanes and erosion. Go see them before they disappear into the sea forever!

sharp shell = Calusa weapon

Awesome Shelling Beach

The birds and creatures on **Keewaydin Island** outnumber the people about two million to one. Actually, we made this number up, but you get the idea. Like Cape Romano, it has beautiful sand and great shelling. Pay attention and you might see a **giant spiny-tail iguana** more than three feet long. Don't worry – they're vegetarians and wouldn't find you at all tasty.

Tigertail Beach

Why didn't they name it Panthertail, when we have panthers in the wild here, but no tigers? Because Tiger Tail is an **important Native American name** here, including Chief Tigertail of the Seminole tribe and Buffalo Tiger, a founder of the Miccosukee tribe. Tigertail Beach Park is a most excellent place to spend a day. There's a great beach for playing and castle-building, paddleboards, kayaks and water toys to rent, a playground, boardwalks across the dunes (look for gopher tortoises!), picnic tables, grills, beach cabanas, a snack bar, and even a butterfly garden.

Beautiful Spit

Not that kind, silly. "Spit" also means an island that once was part of the mainland. A shallow lagoon now separates Tigertail Beach from Sand Dollar Spit. You can wade or kayak across the lagoon to the island for swimming and shelling.

KEEP OUT
BIRD NESTING AREA

Bird Nesting Areas Are Protected By State and Federal Law. Do Not Enter This Area.

Notice: The Area Behind This Sign Is An Important Bird Nesting Site. Disturbance by Humans or Pets Can Cause Nest Abandonment And Death of Young Birds.

Sand Dollar Spit is an important Florida Critical Wildlife Area, so please respect the protected bird nesting areas.

There's no bridge to Keewaydin or Cape Romano, so hop aboard a **super-fun sightseeing or shelling cruise** from Marco or Naples.

Do you like large, medium or family-size boats? *Calusa Spirit* motor catamaran (medium size) picks up passengers at three Marco locations. The yacht *Marco Island Princess* (large size) sails from Rose Marina. Off the Hook Adventures has family-size sailing catamarans departing from Caxambas Park Marina. *Cool Bean Cruises'* family-size boats sail from Isles of Capri.

Families also can rent pontoon boats at Rose Marina. Three great large boats, *Sweet Liberty* catamaran, the yacht *Naples Princess*, the double decker *Double Sunshine* and others sail from Naples.

What the Sea Bird Sees

Wonder what the Ten Thousand Islands and Everglades look like to a sea bird in flight? Here are two ways to find out.

By Parasail

Drift oh-so-gently above the water in a comfy saddle-sling beneath a rainbow-colored parachute. You might see a shark, or a pelican diving for its lunch. You can parasail solo, or tandem with your bestie. Try it with **Marco Island WaterSports**.

By Helicopter

Big boats look like toys from 500 feet up, on your **Island Hopper Helicopter** tour. Maybe you'll spot dolphins playing, or a giant loggerhead turtle swimming toward her nesting beach. And **WOW!** What a view of the Gulf of Mexico, all the way to the horizon!

Hey kids age 15 and up! Ever consider becoming a helicopter pilot? Try it for real, with Island Hopper Helicopters' Discovery Flight.

"We dolphins are air-breathing mammals, not fish! Even when we're happy, that's not really a smile you see. It's just the way our jaws are designed."

WaveRunner action

For fun, open-water excitement, check out **Full Throttle WaveRunners**. Kids age three and up are welcome. Adults can also rent WaveRunners at the launch site in Caxambas Park.

Polka-dot Batfish?

Imagine a triangle-shaped, polka dotted fish that looks like a bat with warts, with lipstick-colored lips, legs, and a fishing lure on her head. There she is, walking along the sandy seagrass bed with that lure wiggling away. All of a sudden, a delicious-looking shrimp swims by. She puckers up those red lips and whoosh... lunch! **True or false?**

Kevin Bryant

If you said "true," you're right! And that's not the only outrageous creature living in the Rookery Bay National Estuarine Research Reserve. The humongous **mangrove estuary** is home to gazillions of birds and animals. At the **Environmental Learning Center**, you can watch some of them in the aquarium, touch some in the touch tank, and see the skulls and bones of others. Look for manatees from the observation bridge, or walk the **Snail Trail**. There also are guided kayak tours, awesome day and night boat cruises, and special kids programs.

Admission is free for kids on Fridays all summer. ← !!

QUIZ
An estuary is a...

a. stupid made-up word
b. performance stage at Sea World
c. protected place where fresh water from rivers mixes with salt water from the sea

Answer: c

Camp Like a Pirate

What's it like to camp out in the Ten Thousand Islands like the ancient Calusas, pirates and hermits?

Tent camping is free on several islands in the Rookery Bay Reserve. Will you find any Calusa weapons or Spanish doubloons buried in the sand?

istockphoto/Thinkstock

Yak Yak Yak

It's all about the Yak. Kayak, that is. **Kayak Marco** has manatee and dolphin kayak tours, beach-and-picnic tours, sunset and full moon tours. On dark summer nights you can even paddle out to see the bioluminescence, the fireflies of the sea!

Don't worry if you've never kayaked before. It's easy!

Shhhh! Paddle Quietly!

Putting your kayak or canoe in the water where no motors are allowed gives you the best chance of spotting wildlife. That's the idea at **Isles of Capri Paddlecraft Park**. There are covered pavilions, so bring a picnic!

←Manatee

Dolphin Whisperers

Humans love dolphins, and when treated respectfully they certainly seem to love us back. They definitely love eco-guides Captain Ron and Avi (whose nickname is The Dolphin Whisperer), at **Captain Ron's Awesome Everglades Adventures.** Your WaveRunner tour gets you face to face with these friendly show-offs. Don't be surprised if a sweet-natured, curious manatee also swims up to say "hi."

WaveRunner: Ron Hageman

Be a Dolphin Researcher

Seriously! You can be part of the important 10,000 Islands Dolphin Research Project. The research crew aboard **Dolphin Explorer** studies about 200 dolphins in the estuaries around Marco Island. Guess how they recognize them? By the shape and markings on their dorsal fins, and sometimes by scrapes and scars. **Whoever discovers a new member of the pod gets to name it!** The three-hour expedition stops at Keewaydin Island for shelling and swimming, and you get an official Dolphin Researcher patch.

Official Patch

45

Go Fish!

Imagine catching a fish as tall as you are. Lots of kids do! Fish in the estuaries or head into the Gulf of Mexico to look for really huge ones. Several adventure and fishing charters at Rose Marina and in Goodland specialize in families and kids.

Shark Adventure

Want a reel adventure? (Get it? **r-e-e-l!**). **Dreamlander Tours** has a fishing trip that's all about sharks: nurse sharks, blacktip sharks, sand sharks and bonnethead sharks. The captains are environmental scientists. You can take pictures and even touch these mysterious creatures before releasing them. **Okay, they're not cuddly like puppies**, but once you get to know them, you may like them!

"A shark's skin is rough like sandpaper—not smooth like mine!"

Mackle Park
Shoot Hoops, See Movies, Walk the Dog

Big kids: hit the game room, basketball court, or sand volleyball court. Little kids: head for the Kids' Cove playground and water spray park. Collared dogs can play unleashed at **Canine Cove Dog Park.** There are free outdoor movies October to May, and special events for families year-round.

Movie and a Taco

...Or spaghetti or pizza - whatever! Watch the movie while having dinner at Marco Movies.

or an Oreo ice cream sundae?

ADMIT ONE
★ ★ ★ ★
Good only date sold
048211

Pickleball? Really?

Yep, it's a real game - a fun mishmash of ping-pong, badminton and tennis. So easy, even your parents can play. Try pickleball, tennis and more at the **Marco Island Racquet Center.**

47

Beachiest 4th of July Festival Ever!

If you're on Marco for the 4th of July, lucky you! The free all-day beach party has sack races, three-legged races, patriotic swimsuit contests, hot-dog eating, hula hooping, limbo and sandcastle-building contests. And, of course, fireworks!

Goodland: Fishing, Eco-Tours and Weird Human Buzzards

This tiny fishing village seems like a separate island, mostly because it's far from Marco's fancy resorts and neighborhoods, but also because it's a little, well, odd. The best things for families are the excellent eco-tours, fishing charters, and old-fashioned seafood shacks.

← Buzzard Lope Princess

Here's the "weird human buzzard" **part:**
On Sunday afternoons, people jump onto the outdoor stage at Stan's Idle Hour Restaurant and do a most peculiar dance called the **Buzzard Lope**. Each year, at the Mullet Festival, women and girls show up in outrageous buzzard costumes. They even crown a Buzzard Lope Queen and Princess.

With live rock and country bands, dock and a **wacky souvenir shop**, Stan's is definitely an interesting lunch stop for Sunday boaters.

Q. Does the Everglades have seasons?

A.
You bet it does! Our colors change here, too! For one thing, summer rains turn the sawgrass prairies as green as Kermit the Frog. In dry winter months, they turn golden. Which is more splendiferous? That's a tough question!

Find out more →

THE EVERGLADES
ALLIGATORS, PANTHERS AND BIRDS, OH MY!

This enchanted wilderness has many secrets, like a beautiful white ghost that's not the least bit spooky and raptors descended from dinosaurs. It's a wild place where alligators, panthers and bears live free, and brown swamp water tastes dee-licious – honest!

You can paddle through mysterious mangrove tunnels, slog up to your knees in a swamp, rumble through the outback on a swamp buggy, or swoosh like a hurricane in a wild airboat ride. Is that all? No way! **Put on your adventure shoes** and take a look!

panther: Dennis Axer
great egret: Purestock/Thinkstock

Airboat!

Know what the first Everglades airboats were made of? Old Model T Ford parts, airplane engines and **humongous propellers**. Airboats can push through the wet sawgrass prairies in just three inches of water! **Seminole and Miccosukee Indians** still go hunting and fishing in flat-bottom airboats.

Florida has at least **a million gators**. The biggest population is right here in the Everglades! And here's something to amaze your friends: The Everglades is the only place on earth where alligators and crocodiles share the same habitat.

But not exactly BFFs

A newspaper reporter named Marjory Stoneman Douglas came up with the perfect name: **River of Grass.** You can see why!

She did more than anyone in history to protect this amazing wilderness from being destroyed.

Helped save the Everglades!

River of Grass

Manatee Sightings!

After you get a selfie with the creatures on this Everglades mural at the **Big Cypress Swamp Welcome Center**, go inside to see the cool exhibits. Then, go out to the boardwalk, meet the rangers and look for manatees. **It's free!**

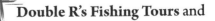

Vegetarian ↑

Frank Brinker

Double R's Fishing Tours and

Manatee Sightseeing Eco Adventures both

have fun pontoon boat tours at Port of the Islands Resort.

Free boardwalk in Fakahatchee Strand ends at a deep, dark alligator hole! It's right on Highway 41 next to the Indian Village, and **it's free!**

To a biologist, a hammock is a **small, shady forest** in the middle of marshlands.

Don't sleep in this hammock!
(unless you're a panther or something)

Kids ride free on Captain Steve's Swamp Buggy Adventures.

Captain Steve – 6th generation Gladesman.

Q. Who are the Gladesmen?

A. Descendents of the hunters, fishermen and moonshiners who lived in camps deep in the alligator-infested swamps, hammocks and prairies of the Everglades. Many Gladesmen are now naturalist guides who give tours into the **Big Cypress Preserve** to look for deer, panther and bear tracks - and maybe the creatures they belong to!

← bear track!

QUIZ
Gladesmen were born in
a. The Everglades
b. A fancy hotel in Paris
c. New York City

Answer: a

Can you believe that the Everglades start just 30 minutes from Marco Island and 45 minutes from Naples?

The **Gulf Coast Visitor Center** has a nature center, camping information, free ranger talks and guided paddling, bike and walking tours. Bring your own kayak, canoe or bike or rent one. You also can sign up in the gift shop for sightseeing and wildlife tours with **Everglades National Park Boat Tours.**

← half price for kids under 12

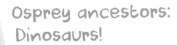

Osprey ancestors: Dinosaurs!

No wonder these **raptors** are fierce! Just watch them go crashing feet-first into the water to catch their prey with **super-sharp talons.** Look for huge osprey stick-nests on top of dead treetops and channel markers.

Hey Kids! Want to see the Everglades from the air? Check out Wings Aero Tours at Everglades City Airpark.

Everglades City

Barron Collier built a fishing and hunting lodge in the Everglades and loved it so much he built a fancy, modern town around it and called it Everglade. Then he hired 2,000 men to finish the road from Tampa to Miami through the boggy, buggy swamps. It's called the Tamiami Trail.

← Worst job ever!

Get it? TAMpa - MIAMI!

Now it's Everglades City, and it's not fancy anymore (that's a good thing!). Instead, it's the number one place to start your Everglades eco-adventures. The workers' bunkhouse is now the **Ivey House Eco-Lodge and Everglades Adventures Company.** Barron Collier's old hunting lodge is now the **Rod and Gun Club,** a way-cool restaurant.

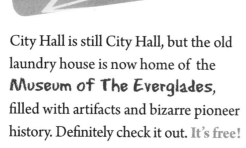

City Hall is still City Hall, but the old laundry house is now home of the **Museum of The Everglades,** filled with artifacts and bizarre pioneer history. Definitely check it out. **It's free!**

Everglades City is airboat heaven!

There's **Captain Jack's**, **Jungle Erv's**, **Captain Mitch**, **Captain Bruce** and **Speedy's**, just for starters. **Totch's Everglades Island Airboat Tours** goes to the old island camp of **famous alligator hunter Totch Brown.**

How brave are you? Check out the frog legs at Camellia Street Grill

One claw only!

Everglades City is the **stone crab capital of the world!** Crabbers can take only one claw, and then must release the crab back into the water to grow a new one. Have a taste during stone crab season, October - May, at one of our super-fun stone crab and seafood festivals!

But why wait? If you're in the mood for stone crab claws, blue crab, **juicy oysters**, **fried frog legs** or really, really, really fresh fish, you're in the right town. And don't forget the Key lime pie.

Frog legs at Miller's World Famous Oyster House →→

55

Walking islands

The roots of red mangroves look like humongous spider legs walking through the creek. They make **awesome tunnels** so low you sometimes have to duck your head to get through! Sign up at **Everglades Area Tours** for a naturalist-guided kayak tour through the tunnels and grasslands.

Do you see ➚
what we see?

You're headed here

Super fun guide

Fast boat

Your kayak goes here

You ride here

Everglades Area Tours.com

239-695-3633

Check out the **boat-assisted kayak trips**, too! A big boat takes you and the kayaks to some outer islands where you can paddle, **beachcomb**, and **muck around in the mud flats** for baby starfish, horseshoe crabs and other creatures. Want more? Ask about **Captain Don's camping adventures!**

Indian Trading Post

100 years ago, Chokoloskee Island was like the **Wild West**, just a different kind of frontier. Pioneers, fishermen, alligator hunters, Indians, Gladesmen–even **outlaws and hermits**–came by boat and dugout canoe to Ted Smallwood's store to trade animal hides, fur, and alligator meat for supplies.

Smallwood's Store is a museum now, but it feels just like it did then. You'll even see **old Ted**, still sitting in his favorite rocking chair!

People say the store is **haunted by the ghosts** of outlaws – and maybe that old pirate, Juan Gomez. **Movie crews are always coming around**, hoping to film a ghost.

Ghosts!?!

In the gift shop you can buy all kinds of Everglades stuff, and sign up for the exciting **Smallwood Store Boat Tour.** The captain knows the way to the bird rookeries and other **secret places in the Ten Thousand Islands.**

Whoa!
Giant white pelicans have ten-foot wingspans!

Ghost hunters!

oh no, not just one day!

Would you choose to **fly like the wind** through the River of Grass on an airboat? Rattle, rumble and roll through the cypress forest in a swamp buggy? Maybe you'd rather see a fearless alligator wrestler put his face practically inside the creatures' jaws, or get eyeball to eyeball with a gazillion slithering alligators.

Surprise! At **Wooten's Everglades Airboat Tours** you can do ALL those things, say hi to a rattlesnake or two, and still have time for a picnic.

great ride for deer sightings!

Everglades adventure?

Waaaaay before you were born, a family of Gladesmen named Wooten decided to see if any tourists might want to take airboat rides, and maybe see some alligators. They put a big sign up on the highway to see if anyone would come.

Well, of course everyone did! And they still do. Now there's tons more to see. You can't miss the giant red and yellow sign, just east of Everglades City on U.S. 41.

Who wants to hug a baby gator?

Best deal: free live alligator show and animal sanctuary with airboat and swamp buggy combo!

Dan Laursen

I bazillion and one

I bazillion and two

I bazillion and three

Seminole War at Billie Swamp Safari!

What??? The U.S. is STILL trying to take over Indian land? Okay, it's just acting, but if that looks like musket-fire to you, you're right. At the annual **Big Cypress Shootout** you can watch Seminole warriors **battle the U.S. militia**, see the war camps, taste Seminole food, buy Indian crafts, and watch snake handlers, alligator wrestlers and tribal dancers.

Spoiler alert! The Indians win. The Seminoles are the only Indians who were never defeated by the United States. That's why they're called the **Unconquered People.**

All year long, Billie Swamp Safari has critter shows, airboat rides and swamp buggy eco-tours. Be sure to taste some gator tail nuggets and **Seminole fry bread** in the Swamp Water Café. You can even camp out in a native-style thatched-roof chickee, go on a night buggy ride, and hear old Seminole legends around the campfire.

Fry bread

Cool birthday sleepover idea!

Ah-Tah-Thi-Ki Seminole Indian Museum

Lots to do here! See the life-size Seminole scenes, watch
the movie *We Seminoles*, and take the boardwalk through
the cypress dome, past the ceremonial grounds, to the
living Seminole village.

Chickee: It's not what you might think.

Many Seminoles still live in traditional open-sided huts
with palm frond roofs. Most chickees around Naples,
Marco Island and
the Everglades were
built by members of
the Seminole tribe.

Not! →

istockphoto/Thinkstock

Chickee Chobee ("big chickee") at
Trail Lakes Campground in Ochopee is perfect
for a family of five. It even has a loft!

Skunk Ape?

Do you believe in Bigfoot? Well, this 7 foot-tall, 350-pound creature that smells like a skunk could be its Everglades cousin. It stinks because it wallows around in alligator holes (which are full of swamp gas), eats too many **lima beans**, and never bathes.

Uh, Really?? ↗

You can go on a swamp expedition and get an official skunk ape T-shirt at the **Skunk Ape Headquarters** in Ochopee.

← *weird job alert: Head Skunk Ape Researcher!*

Pythons?

Yep. HUGE ones. There may be thousands of Burmese pythons in the Everglades, but hardly anybody sees one in the wild, because they keep to themselves. Goldie, here, is 30 feet long and **weighs 300 pounds**. She lives at the Skunk Ape Headquarters.

really shallow water! ↓

Q. How amazing would it be to go pole boating with a real Gladesman deep in the swamps, across the open grass prairies and into the mangrove tunnels, the old Everglades way?

A. Totally amazing! Check out Everglades Adventure Tours at the Skunk Ape Headquarters.

Plumes

Back when ladies wore outrageous bird-feather hats, hunters killed five million egrets and herons every single year to sell their feathers. Imagine how many gazillion birds once lived here!

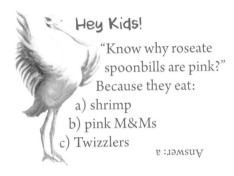

Hey Kids!

"Know why roseate spoonbills are pink?" Because they eat:

a) shrimp
b) pink M&Ms
c) Twizzlers

Answer: a

No-See-Ums

These insects are so tiny you can't see them, but you sure can feel their nasty bites – especially after a rain, near water and just before sunset.

Swamp Angels
(that's a mosquito joke)

If you're exploring the 'glades in summer without your repellant, you definitely won't be calling these annoying creatures angels. Here's a nice surprise: mosquitoes don't hang out in cypress swamps because certain plants and fish like to eat them.

Did you know that only female mosquitoes bite?

Dark Night Stargazing

Attention future astronauts and astronomers! On super-dark nights, the **Everglades Astronomical Society** sets up **gigantic telescopes** on the prairie of Big Cypress National Park and at Collier-Seminole State Park to look at meteors, planets and nebulas. They have ladders so even little kids can see!

Wow! Andromeda Galaxy!

You can book a private night of stargazing with **Linda's Stargazing Adventures**. Linda is a Florida Master Naturalist, astronomer and storyteller. If you're camping, she'll come to your campsite, and even bring the s'mores!

Oooh, graham crackers, marshmallows and chocolate: Best campfire treat ever!

Why did the gator cross the road?

To get to the gator on the other side!

Never try to feed an alligator. Their eyes aren't so good and sometimes they can't tell a hand from a nice juicy frog.

Amazon of North America

You know about the Amazon rainforest, right? It's the largest rainforest on the planet. Well, **Fakahatchee Strand is America's Amazon!** This awesome bald cypress swamp forest is loaded with rare tropical plants, clear water, and lots of creatures like **black bears**, **Florida panthers**, **white tailed deer** and **tropical snakes.**

You can sign up to go slogging through the swamp with a park naturalist. It's such outrageous fun, even grownups love it! Wear your grungy shoes and bring dry clothes.

↖Best excuse ever to get dirty!

A Ghost in the Swamp

People come to Fakahatchee Strand State Preserve from all over the world to look for the super-rare ghost orchid. It's called "ghost" because it's white and floaty-looking. It also looks like a **tiny ballerina.** She usually blooms only once a year, but sometimes she makes an extra appearance!

Deer Alert!

Janes Scenic Drive, an old logging road in Fakahatchee Strand, is a great place to watch for wildlife. Maybe even a panther.

The Tree's Knees

What are those pointy things poking out of the water beside the cypress trees? Cypress knees! They shoot up from the tree's roots to help it breathe, kind of like a snorkel!

Corey Billie's Airboat Rides

The Billie family, descendants of a Seminole chief, gives exciting airboat tours in their private wilderness land at the edge of the Fakahatchee Strand Preserve. It's the airboat attraction closest to Naples and Marco Island.

Smallest Post Office!

This teeny, tiny post office is smaller than a backyard playhouse! Only one person can fit inside at a time! It's right on U.S. 41 in Ochopee.

Clyde Butcher

The world's most famous **Everglades photographer** loves sloshing around taking pictures in the deep, dark **Big Cypress Swamp.** You can join one of his super-fun naturalist-guided walks that start right behind his **Big Cypress Gallery** in Ochopee. People who really, REALLY love the swamp can even rent his **personal swamp cottage**, where the backyard critters are alligators.

Miccosukee Festival

The Miccosukee Indian Village is closer to Miami than Naples, but worth the drive during its **Indian Arts and Crafts Festival** each December. Lots of alligator wrestling, dancing, Indian food, art and crafts and Indian-guided airboat rides.

Pssst!
Best Scenic Roads in Big Cypress!

Early mornings and late afternoons are when all kinds of wildlife hang out on **Loop Road** (27-mile ride) and **Turner River Road** (17-mile ride). Look for deer, alligators, snakes, bald eagles, big wading birds and even a panther or black bear. The gravel roads sometimes get flooded in summer. Ask about conditions at the Big Cypress Visitor Center. ⬅ bumpy ride alert!

Collier-Seminole State Park

Who knew such an awesome wilderness could be just 17 miles from a modern city? There's camping (pets allowed!), nature trails, bicycle and mountain bike trails, kayaking, saltwater and freshwater fishing, Junior Ranger programs, and even moonlight canoe tours.

Sup-fari

It's the latest thing at Collier-Seminole State Park! You go stand-up-paddleboarding in the swamp with real Gladesmen. You won't believe how close you can get to birds and wildlife! Collier-Seminole Nature Tours has other cool tours, too, 7 days a week.

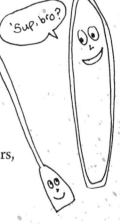

'Sup, bro?

Fishing: Number 1 in the World!

Is a **million acres of water** in the backcountry of the Everglades and the Ten Thousand Islands enough to find some great fish? ESPN said Chokoloskee Island is the number one saltwater fly-fishing destination in the entire world! One big magazine even called Everglades City Captain Steve Huff the best fishing guide alive! It's hard to get Captain Steve unless you want to wait a year, but you'll have lots of fun with **Captain Bruce Hitchcock** (No Free Lunch Charters), **Captain Charles Wright** (Chokoloskee Charters), **Captain Rodney Raffield** (Backcountry Fishing Experience), **Captain Pete Rapps**, and all the other **awesome Everglades fishing guides.** Info at Everglades City Welcome Center

FESTIVALS!

PARADES!

January
Southwest Florida Nature Festival, Rookery Bay mi
Martin Luther King Day Parade, 5th Avenue S. n
New Year's Art Fair, 5th Avenue S. n
Mullet Festival, Goodland mi
Pets on Third, 3rd Street S. n

February
Everglades City Seafood Festival
World Wetlands Day, Corkscrew Swamp Sanctuary n

March
Marco Island Seafood Festival
St. Patrick's Day Parade, Old Naples
Big Cypress Shootout, Billie Swamp Safari e
Old Florida Festival, Collier County Museum n

April
Balloons Over Paradise, Immokalee
Taste of Collier, Bayfront n
Taste of Marco, Esplanade mi

May
Great Dock Canoe Race, Crayton Cove n
Mother's Day! Moms get in free at many attractions!

June
Father's Day! Dads get in free at many attractions!
Early 4th of July Fireworks, Everglades City

July
4th of July Parade, Fifth Avenue S. n
4th of July Fireworks, Naples Pier
Uncle Sam's 4th of July Sand Jam & Fireworks, Marco
Ice Cream Social, ski show & fireworks, Sugden Park n

mi = Marco Island
n = Naples
e = Everglades

ice cream: istockphoto/Thinkstock

FIREWORKS!

October

Halloween Spooktacular, 5th Avenue S. n

Sunflower Festival, Pepper Ranch, Immokalee

Stone Crab Festival n

Swamp Buggy Parade and Races n

August and September

Awesome summer discounts and freebies for kids!

November

Turkey Trot 5K for Kids, Cambier Park n

Grand Illuminations, Santa & snow, Village on Venetian Bay n

Florida Panther Festival, North Collier Regional Park n

Christmas Tree Lighting, Veterans' Park mi

Celebration of Lights and Christmas on 3rd Street S. n

December

Tuba Christmas, 5th Avenue S. n

Christmas Parade, 5th Avenue S. n

Canine Christmas Parade, Esplanade mi

Marco Island Boat Parade and Street Parade

Naples Boat Parades, Naples Bay and Venetian Bay

Christmas Walk, Tree Lighting & Santa, 5th Avenue S. n

Swamp Heritage Festival, Big Cypress National Preserve e

New Year's Eve Fireworks, Naples Pier and Sugden Park n

Tell the grownups! Some years, an event can be either at the end of one month or the beginning of the next month. Always check the local listing.

Jennifer Brinkman

A bazillion thanks!
To the awesome peeps who helped make this book happen.

WISE ONES

To my many mentors, technical gurus and fellow authors for generously sharing your wisdom and encouragement: **Mayor John Sorey, Susan McManus, Jessica Olson,** Buzzy Ford, **Michelle Pirre, Steve Trotter, Kristen Houghton,** and so many others. You know who you are.

I'm grateful to **Brian Holley,** Kara Laufer, **Tim Tetzlaff, Karysia Demarest,** Aashish Patel, **Mike Thrasher, Stacey Thrasher, Jenny Foegen, Serina Williams** and Chris Dupree for taking a leap of faith on behalf of your organizations to become Star Attraction sponsors.

SIDEKICK

To **Linda Jacobson:** Astronomer, passionate environmentalist, Florida Master Naturalist, hiking and camping guide, nature photographer and **intrepid researcher.** I'm so glad our paths crossed that early dawn in the Fakahatchee Strand.

ART PEEPS

To Terri Rickman, for your super-fun cover design and illustrations. To my design team: Judy Fernandez, for painting bright splashes of joyfulness throughout the book; design wizard **Kerry Fischel,** and talented designer Sharon Hood for your amazing ability to see so clearly through my lens.

GRANDMOTHERS & OTHER SUPER-BEINGS

To all the grandparents, parents, aunts, uncles, teachers, home-schoolers, youth leaders, and other grownups who have been asking for this book for so long. Thanks for the inspiration and insights into the hearts and minds of your amazing kids.

TASTE TESTER & SUCH

To Randy Simmons: no words are good enough. Thank you for sharing the adventures, for putting a gazillion miles on your odometer, for taste-testing fried frog legs when I wasn't up to the task; for proofing and re-proofing with your incredible eagle eye. Your presence is on every page.

...KTB

Every effort was made to assure correct information, websites and phone numbers. We welcome updates, and news of exciting new adventures and attractions. Email us at mostlykidsguides@gmail.com • (239) 595-9026 • www.mostlykidsguides.com

STAR ATTRACTIONS

With gratitude to the leaders at these top family attractions for believing in this book and supporting our First Edition. You're a big part of the reason the Paradise Coast is an awesome place for kids, and you just keep making it better.

Thanks to Jack Wert, JoNell Modys and Debi DeBenedetto of the Naples, Marco Island, Everglades Convention & Visitor's Bureau, for believing in this book from the beginning, reinforcing Collier County's commitment to family tourism.

Getting Your Bearings

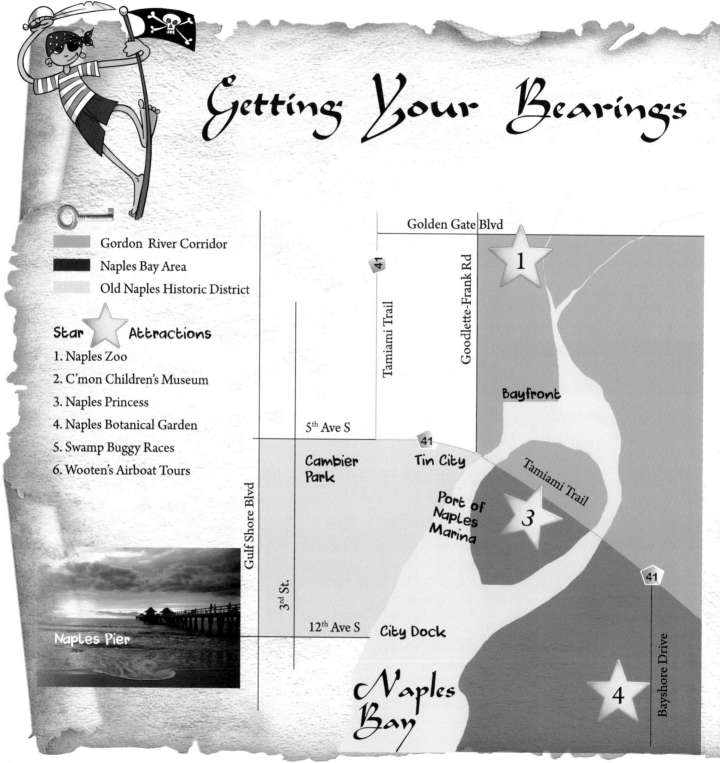

Gordon River Corridor
Naples Bay Area
Old Naples Historic District

Star Attractions

1. Naples Zoo
2. C'mon Children's Museum
3. Naples Princess
4. Naples Botanical Garden
5. Swamp Buggy Races
6. Wooten's Airboat Tours

Golden Gate Blvd

Goodlette-Frank Rd

Tamiami Trail

41

Bayfront

5th Ave S

41

Tin City

Cambier Park

Tamiami Trail

Port of Naples Marina

3

Gulf Shore Blvd

3rd St.

41

Naples Pier

12th Ave S

City Dock

Bayshore Drive

Naples Bay

4

Barefoot Beach

111th Ave N

Delnor-Wiggins Beach

Vanderbilt Beach

41

Clam Pass Beach

Seagate Dr

Lowdermilk Beach

Pier

Old Naples

Naples Bay

Keewaydin Isl

Rookery Bay

Naples

Golden Gate Blvd

Goodlette-Frank Rd

Vanderbilt Beach Rd

Immokalee Rd

2

Pine Ridge Rd

Livingston Rd

Airport-Pulling Rd

75

Corkscrew Swamp   CREW

Lake Trafford

Immokalee

951

Alligator Alley

75

Picayune Strand

29

1

Collier County Museum

41

3

4

Marco Island

Collier Blvd

Tamiami

92

5

Collier-Seminole State Park

Trail

Fakahatchee Strand

41

Big Cypress Swamp

6   Ochopee

Tigertail Beach

Port of the Islands

Everglades

10,000 Islands ➜

Everglades City

Chokoloskee

Everglades National Park

Map not to scale

TIME'S A'WASTN' MATEYS! GET GOING!

A
A & B Charters aandbcharters.com (877) 263-2320
Ah-Tah-Thi-Ki Seminole Indian Museum ahtahthiki.com (877) 902-1113
Artis—Naples artisnaples.org (239) 597-1900

B
Balloons Over Paradise seminoleimmokaleecasino.com/event/balloons-over-paradise
Big Cypress National Preserve nps.gov/bicy (239) 695-2000
Big Cypress Shootout bcshootout.com (800) 949-6101
Big Cypress Swamp Welcome Center nps.gov/bicy (239) 695-4758
Billie Swamp Safari swampsafari.com (863) 983-6101

C
Calusa Spirit marcoislandwatersports.com (239) 642-2359
Cambier Park naplesgov.com (239) 213-3058; Tennis (239) 213-3060
Captain Jack's Airboat Tours captainjacksairboattours.com (239) 695-4400
Captain Ron's Awesome Everglades Adventures evergladesjetskitours.com (239) 777-9975
Captain Steve's Swamp Buggy captainstevesswampbuggyadventures.com (239) 695-2186
Central Bark (City of Naples Dog Park) naplesgov.com (239) 213-7120
Charlene's Carriage Tours charlenesclassiccarriages.com (239) 246-0956
Clyde Butcher's swamp walks clydebutchersbigcypressgallery.com (239) 695-2428
C'mon Golisano Children's Museum cmon.org (239) 514-0084
Collier County Library programs collierlibrary.org (239) 593-0334
Collier County Museum colliermuseums.com (239) 252-8476
Collier Family Farms collierfamilyfarms.com (239) 207-5231
Collier Seminole Nature Tours collierseminole.com (239) 790-1407
Collier Seminole State Park floridastateparks.org/collierseminole (239) 394-3397
Conservancy of Southwest Florida conservancy.org (239) 262-0304
Cool Beans Cruises coolbeanscruises.com (239) 777-0020
Coral Cay Adventure Golf coralcaygolf.com (239) 793-4999
Corey Billie Airboat Rides cbairboatrides.com (239) 389-7433
Corkscrew Swamp Sanctuary corkscrew.audubon.org (239) 348-9151
Crayton Cove naplescraytoncove.com (239) 404-5014
CREW crewtrust.org (239) 657-2253

D

Dolphin Explorer dolphin-explorer.com (239) 642-6899
Double R's Fishing & Tour Co. doublersfishingandtours.com (239) 642-9779
Double Sunshine purenaples.com (239) 263-4949
Dreamlander Tours dreamlandertours.com (239) 331-3775

E

Everglades Adventure Tours evergladesadventuretours.com (561) 985-8207
Everglades Area Tours evergladesareatours.com (239) 695-3633
Everglades Astronomical Society naples.net/clubs/eas
Everglades Nat'l Park Boat Tours evergladesnationalparkboattoursgulfcoast.com (239) 695-2591
Everglades National Park Visitor Center nps.gov/ever (239) 695-3311
Extreme Family Fun Spot extremefamilyfunspot.com (239) 774-0061

F

Fakahatchee Strand Preserve State Park floridastateparks.org/fakahatcheestrand (239) 695-4593
Fifth Avenue South fifthavenuesouth.com (239) 692-8436
Fleischmann Park naplesgov.com (239) 213-3020
Florida Adrenaline swfladrenaline.com (239) 849-0283
Florida Sports Park thefloridasportspark.com (239) 774-2701
Florida State Parks floridastateparks.org
Full Throttle WaveRunners fullthrottlewaverunners.com (239) 728-8919

G–H

Gordon River Greenway gordonrivergreenway.org
Holocaust Museum & Education Center holocaustmuseumswfl.org (239) 263-9200

I–J

Immokalee Pioneer Museum at Roberts Ranch colliermuseums.com (239) 658-2466
Island Hoppers Aerial Adventures ravenair.net (239) 777-4046
Isles of Capri Paddlecraft Park (see Rookerybay.org)
Ivey House/Everglades Adventures evergladesadventures.com (239) 695-3299
Jet Boat Naples purenaples.com (239) 263-4949
Jungle Erv's Airboat World jungleervairboatworld.com (877) 695-2820
Junior Ranger Programs nps.gov/bicy or floridastateparks.org

K–L

Kayak Marco Island kayakmarco.com (239) 288-0210
Kowiachobee Animal Preserve kowia.com (239) 352-5387
Lady Brett purenaples.com (239) 263-4949
Lake Trafford Marina laketrafford.com (239) 657-2214
Linda's Stargazing Adventures astronomygal.com (239) 851-7827

M

M&H Stables mhstables.com (239) 455-8764
Mackle Park cityofmarcoisland.com (239) 642-0575
Manatee Sightseeing Eco Adventure see-manatees.com (239) 642-8818
Marco Golf and Garden marcogolfandgarden.com (239) 970-0561
Marco Island Chamber of Commerce marcoislandchamber.org (239) 394-7549
Marco Island Historical Museum colliermuseums.com (239) 642-1440
Marco Island Princess themarcoislandprincess.com (239) 642-5415
Marco Island Racquet Center marco-island-tennis.com (239) 394-5454
Marco Island Watersports marcoislandwatersports.com (239) 642-2359
Marco Movies marcomovies.com (239) 642-1111
Miccosukee Tribe of Indians miccosukee.com (305) 480-1924
Museum of the Everglades colliermuseums.com (239) 695-0008

N

Naples Bay Water Shuttle naplesbaywatershuttle.com (239) 206-0160
Naples Bicycle Tours naplesbicycletours.com (239) 825-6344
Naples Botanical Garden naplesgarden.org (239) 643-7275
Naples Chocolate Stroll napleschocolatestroll.com (239) 653-7933
Naples Depot Museum colliermuseums.com (239) 262-6525
Naples Explorer purenaples.com (239) 263-4949
Naples Marina and Excursions cruisefishdive.com (239) 592-1200
Naples Princess naplesprincesscruises.com (239) 649-2275
Naples Segway Tours extremefamilyfunspot.com (239) 774-0061
Naples Train Museum naplestrainmuseum.org (239) 262-1776
Naples Trolley Tours naplestrolleytours.com (239) 262-7300
Naples Zoo at Caribbean Gardens napleszoo.com (239) 262-5409
National Park Service nps.gov
No Free Lunch Charters backcountryfishing.net (239) 695-2172
North Collier Regional Park colliergov.net (239) 252-4000

O

Old Florida Festival oldfloridafestival.com (239) 252-8476
Orange Jeep Tours orangejeeptours.com (239) 434-5337

P

Palm Cottage napleshistoricalsociety.org (239) 261-8164
Paradise Coast Blueway paradisecoastblueway.com
Pepper Ranch Preserve colliergov.net (239) 657-1999
Port of the Islands Fishing and Tours doublersfishingandtours.com (239) 642-9779

Thinkstock

Port of the Islands Manatee Tour see-manatees.com (239) 642-8818

Pure Naples purenaples.com (239) 263-4949

R

Revs Institute revsinstitute.org (239) 687-7387

Rookery Bay Environmental Learning Center rookerybay.org (239) 530-5940

Rose Marina rosemarina.com (239) 394-2502

Rover Run, Veterans Community Park, Naples colliergov.net (239) 566-2367

S

Scuba Marco scubamarco.com (239) 389-7889

Sea Excursions seaexcursions.com (239) 642-6400

Segway of Naples Tours segwayofnaples.com (239) 262-7205

Shy Wolf Sanctuary shywolfsanctuary.com (239) 455-1698

Six Chuter Charters sixchutercharters.com (239) 389-1575

Skunk Ape Research Headquarters skunkape.info (239) 695-2275

Smallwood Boat Tours smallwoodstoreboattour.com (239) 695-0016

Smallwood Store smallwoodstore.com (239) 695-2989

Stan's Idle Hour stansidlehour.net (230) 394-3041

Sugden Theatre naplesplayers.org (239) 263-7990

Sugden Regional Park colliergov.net (239) 793-4414

Sun & Fun Lagoon napleswaterpark.com (239) 252-4021

Swamp Buggy Races thefloridasportspark.com (239) 774-2701

Sweet Liberty sweetliberty.com (239) 793-3525

T

Ten Thousand Islands National Wildlife Refuge fws.gov/refuges (239) 353-8442

The Edge Johnny Nocera Skate Park naplesgov.com (239) 213-3020

Third Street South thirdstreetsouth.com (239) 434-6533

Tin City tin-city.com (239) 262-4200

Totch's Island Airboat Tours airboateverglades.com (239) 695-2333

Trail Lakes Campground evergladescamping.net (239) 790-1407

U–V

U.S Fish & Wildlife Service myfwc.com (850) 488-4676

Veterans Community Park Naples colliergov.net (239) 566-2367

Veterans' Community Park Marco Island cityofmarcoisland.com (239) 642-0575

W

Wings Ten Thousand Islands Aero Tours wingsaerotours.com (239) 695-3296

Wooten's Everglades Adventures wootenseverglades.com (239) 695-2781

MAJOR BEACHES AND BEACH PARKS WITH FACILITIES

On-site facility phone numbers listed when available

Barefoot Beach Preserve County Park, 505 Barefoot Beach Blvd., Naples
  (Access gate at 5901 Bonita Beach Road, Bonita Springs)

Clam Pass Beach Park 465 Seagate Dr., Naples
Delnor Wiggins Pass State Park 11135 Gulfshore Dr., Naples (239) 597-6196
Lowdermilk Beach Park 1301 Gulf Shore Blvd., Naples
Naples Pier 25 12th Ave. S., Naples
Tigertail Beach 490 Hernando Dr., Marco Island (239) 642-8414
Vanderbilt Beach 100 Vanderbilt Beach Rd., Naples

VISITOR INFORMATION

Collier County
Collier County Convention & Visitors Bureau paradisecoast.com (800) 688-3600
Collier County Parks and Recreation colliergov.net (239) 252-4000
Naples, Marco Island, Everglades Convention & Visitors Bureau
  paradisecoast.com (800) 688-3600 (239) 252-2384

Naples
City of Naples naplesgov.com (239) 213-1000
Naples Parks & Recreation naplesgov.com (239) 213-1000
Greater Naples Chamber of Commerce Visitor Center
  napleschamber.org (239) 262-6376

Naples Historical Society napleshistoricalsociety.org (239) 261-8164
Naples Preserve & Hedges Family Eco-Center naplesgov.com (239) 261-4290

Marco Island
City of Marco Island cityofmarcoisland.com (239) 389 5000
Marco Island Chamber of Commerce marcoislandchamber.org (239) 394-7549

Everglades City
  Everglades City florida-everglades.com (239) 821-5219
  Everglades City Welcome Center evergladeschamber.com (239) 695-3941

About the Author

Karen T. Bartlett is an award-winning writer, photographer, author of 11 destination **travel books**, and hundreds of travel articles and photos that have been published in magazines and **newspapers** in several countries.

She's a member of the American Society of Media Photographers (ASMP) and the Society of American Travel Writers (SATW).

She was born in Savannah, Georgia, and has a funny Southern accent. Before she became an author, she was president of a leading **public relations** agency in Atlanta, Georgia with big-shot clients like Coca Cola USA, Hartsfield Atlanta International Airport, Coldwell Banker, and SAS Airlines. Then she became the **travel editor** of *Gulfshore Life* (a fancy Naples magazine), and a freelance writer/photographer for the *Toronto Star* (Canada's largest newspaper), and several way-cool Caribbean travel magazines.

When her two (now grown up) children were small, the family moved to Naples, Florida, and the adventures began!

Vanessa Rogers

As Adventurer in Chief of *A (mostly) Kids' Guide to Naples, Marco Island & The Everglades,* she writes from the point of view of a **reporter**, a **storyteller**, and **especially a mom**.

She loves to dance, get muddy in the swamp, **eat chocolate ice cream** and **get emails** from her readers.

CPSIA information can be obtained at www.ICGtesting.com
Printed in the USA
LVIW01n1321300816
502484LV00007B/24

* 9 7 8 0 9 9 0 9 7 3 1 0 2 *